Looking Through A Mirror

Nikhita Kalluri

BookLeaf Publishing

India | USA | UK

Presentation by *BookLeaf Publishing*

Web: www.bookleafpub.com

E-mail: info@bookleafpub.com

ISBN: 9789357214872

First edition 2022

For all who have shined their light,

spoken their truth

The world is a better place

because of you

PREFACE

"Only from the heart can you touch the sky."
- Rumi

"Let us fill our hearts with our own compassion
- towards ourselves and towards all beings."
- Thich Nhat Hanh

"May all beings everywhere be happy and free,
and may the thoughts, words, and actions of my
own life contribute in some way to that
happiness and to that freedom for all."
लोकाः समस्ताः सुखिनो भवन्तु
- Sanskrit Mantra

"The journey of a thousand miles begins with
one step."
- Lao Tzu

— ~ — ~ — ~ —

There it was
The most brilliant light
Illumination
at its purest

So intense
For one moment
a single point in time
we had awakened
From the deepest slumbers
of an ubiquitous ignorance

— ~ — ~ — ~ —

And like a wisp of smoke
it faded away

kings and queens

We had the world in our hands
we ruled it
wild and free
Back when we thought
oblivion was bliss

But then we lost it
for the wears and tears
of this world
The fluctuations and impermanence
of it all
and when that didn't work
we escaped it too
We couldn't associate ourselves
any longer
With what could never stay
With what could never last
When every time
we thought we made it
We lost it
 time and time again

Now we truly had nothing
but in nothing
we found everything

something of more profundity
something of more depth
Something of truest meaning
Something
that could never be lost

And in it
we lost ourselves
In this dissolution
never wanting to come out
Never needing to come out

- the world really was indestructible

when light turned to shadows

You think
you have fooled the world
But I can see you hiding

I see your fear
Every time
you almost divulge
a hint of emotion
A hint
of something
anything
Beyond
the brick wall of your presence
Beyond
your facade of hardness

I see your dislike
How you are so quick
to condescend
Those who are capable
of exposing a rawness
a realness
Beyond the fathomable

Only in your music

Do you find
a shadow
of what was real

But even then
Music can be used to feel
Or it can be used to numb
And maybe
you are just numbing
what could have been felt

a grand oblivion

Eyes wide open,
but not seeing
what's right in front of us
Wide awake,
but trapped inside a dream
A facade of beauty
Luring us in
to the snake's lair
The most dangerous
of illusions

We have deluded ourselves
into dreams
of a grand oblivion
where the delusion
is oblivion
And oblivion
perpetuates delusion

The human affliction
a cyclic trap
The prison inescapable
Until the desire to escape manifests
or day by day
We go insane

- unbreakable chains

The pretty little glass
and words I said
All it did is hold me back

Reaching for a dream
that never ends
Maybe it was all a lie

- chasing shadows

For even
the stillest of lakes
The most pristine glass
of the most beautiful mirror
Can only project
an inverted reality

- mirrors tell lies

a fragile impermanence

Some days I wake
with the fear
of days wasted away
in oblivion, in ignorance
The brevity of my life
my time days, months, years
in this existence
Smiling upon me
Like this is all a grand game
of creation and dissolution

Some days I feel
A strong sense, an urgency
Pushing me, compelling me
To act
upon my volition solely
in its entirety

To make the most of my life
To live with a wild sense of freedom
To not care what they think
to not care what I make of my living
Because what's the point of it all?

If time will just blow away

all that I have gathered
Only an imprint
of what could have been
Left
for me to rediscover

shifting seasons

The heat ascended upon
the blades of dried grass
Guided only
by the shifting winds

And it burned through
like a wildfire

- heat waves

The shift happened
so fast
All it took
was a single moment
One point
in time

And the leaves fell
nature's brightest colors
Lit up the world
Like the fire
of a thousand suns

- the ripening

The rain came down
Causing all life
as we perceive it
To flee
To hide away
in their momentary homes

Such a time for desolation
The gloomy skies
and ice-old nights
The stormy clouds
obscuring
Even a hint of light

But in cessation
lay
the creation of all growth
And in emptiness
lay
the origination
Of the seen and unseen

- winter nights

Even with the partitioning
Of the seasons
the phases of life
The orbiting
of the planet we inhibit

Around the star
that drives
Our very existence

Is an infinite spectrum
of movement, motion
No parts
Of each whole
ever the same

Like thoughts
like planets
the existence
of the universe itself
Arising and dissolving
Into the vast space
of creation, continuation, dissolution
The void before all happenings

- a cyclic existence

summer days in India

It's my first time here
in two years

I forgot
how thick the air is
I can practically taste it
If it was any thicker
maybe I could hold it

As we drive
windows down, heads out
Drinking everything in
from a world we had missed
The driver is struggling
To find even a crack
In the neverending stream
of complete chaos
Even water
couldn't seep through
in this road
of limbs and machinery
But in the vibrancy
of such motion
is where I find peace

As we swerve past
the different vehicles
Driving between lanes
I see houses
each unique and colorful
Long and tall
With wet clothes
strung across wires
on their rooftops

The temples
are vibrating with music
As they do
At all hours of the day and night

Children are running
happy and carefree
With no supervision
but their own

Neighbors are visiting
the surrounding homes
with sweets to offer
And gossip to share

Everyone
So deeply interconnected
Always present
to lend a hand

or make conversation

In this land
Of friendship and community

- hyderabadi at heart

We were always a team
You and I
You would take me on rides
on your motorcycle
And I would squeal with delight
asking you to go faster and faster
Faster than anyone had possibly moved
in all of time's history
Because I loved the thrill

We would go to the kitchen
when no one was looking
and sneak out sweets
slowly tiptoeing away
Knowing someone would catch us
but that was where the fun lay
Because we did it together

When you picked up your book
I would pick up mine too
and read intently
And when you fell asleep reading

I would watch
amused and lost in thought
all at the same time

When I was upset
you always knew
and we would go
for long walks into the evening
Because you knew that

Just like you
I could walk away hours
miles across the world
With only my mind
to keep me company

Just like you
I never liked to stay inside
for too long
I needed to be out

I would follow you
into the garden
I was like your tail
Watching you water plants
learning about them
as you spoke
which plants are parasites
Which plants grow best together

which plants
bear the sweetest of fruit
and you would pluck one
for me to eat

We would spend summer evenings
engulfed in the aroma
of the sweetest of flowers blooming
as we stood on the rooftop
Plucking jasmines
I would always race up with my sister
seeing who could pluck more
because we wanted to impress you

All these days spent
with a person of such timeless wisdom,
such selfless compassion
I knew that
when it was time to drive away
these memories
Could only last a lifetime

- summers with a grandfather i'm grateful to call
mine

seeing through the fog

Enough space in my mind
To hold the world
The weight of worlds

A lot to hold
A burden even
But still I bear it

Why is it
that I can't let go
The difficulty that comes
The deepness, the weight of it all
As I sink further and further

As I let the external
Control me, drag me
down deeper and deeper

Until I am lost
Seemingly compassion
but not compassion
Not to myself

Within moments
I have sunk

And now I have to gather the whole of myself
To come back to the surface
To breathe

- sinking, drowning, swimming

Why do I fall so quickly
Why am I so quick
to see the good
When it has hurt me before
And it will hurt me again

Until I am unblinded
Until I can see reality
unbiased
As it is

The markings of footsteps
of those who thought
they could walk all over me
getting deeper and deeper
As if I am shrouded in
the softest of sand
Rather than
the most durable of skin

Why is it so hard for me
To break out of cycles
of longing

Longing for a dream
a chance
of what could have been
a possibility
of what could be
When it's all
just an illusion
that I remain forever entangled in
Until forever intersects now
And I can once again
see clearly

- falling in and out

Maybe it's time
to shatter the illusion
of perceived peace

Holding on
to the broken shards of glass
Only creates scars
And putting them together
veils the truth

only human

I thought I knew
all there was to know
But perfection was only an ideal
as unrealistic and unattainable
as all that can be replaced are

I thought I had knowledge of depth
But identification of knowledge
with the fleeting
lacked any profundity
In the flick of a switch
it could disappear
How shallow was that?

I never knew I could fall
as low as I did
I put myself up on a pedestal
and made myself unreachable
When issues arose
I ensured
I couldn't deal with them
Because in my mind
they never existed

What I couldn't see

was the difference
between denying and seeing
Reality
for what it is
Seeing that
What comes must go
But what is, exists
right now eternally

- the moment i was gone

So alone, but never alone
When all that arises into actuality
manifests itself
I finally realize
Control is an illusion

I took hold of the reigns
and charged through life
with infinite ambition,
the ever growing desire
to create the change I wished to see

I spearheaded it
thinking that was the sole method
of transformation
But somewhere along the way
I started losing myself
to the chaos

of the path of action
Until it swallowed me whole

I only emerged
from this quicksand
that pulled me under
Because of a realization
so profound

The burden of the world
was never mine to shoulder

The understanding that
existence occurs
on an infinite spectrum
of creation
in its diverse variations
So too
is all transformation
Interdependent

Control was never the goal
Unreachable and unrealistic
As the infinite perceptions
and the worlds that arise from them
Tend to be

- the illusion of control

The day I realized my mortality
My body was never invincible
like I believed it to be

Why was it
such a shock to me?

Such attachment
to something so fleeting
Was like dying
a thousand times over

When death
of all that arises
is our only
constant companion

- homo deus

when fire burns too bright

We are trapped in a rat race
forced to compete with each other
We are hamsters
on a wheel
Reaching for a finish line
that could never exist

We are drowning in competition
The pressure of life immense
Hardening us, compacting us
at metamorphic intensities

Always hoping
to gain the upper edge
To be at the top
The top of the top
From the most minute
to the most pivotal
An ideal of success
for what it means to live life
A manifestation
of the vitiated energy
Of fire

But when fire burns

with an intensity so bright
with movement uncontrollable
Its only option
is to destroy everything in its path
blinding us in its journey

We have become
our most feared enemy
The burden
of sole existence
Becoming the death of us

Only in ease
Only in the uncaring, unaffected playfulness
of the most unburdened child
Can we truly grapple
the existential problems
of worlds within and without
without the bias of affliction

Only with the lightness and freedom
of the ever-shifting wind
the ever-flowing water
Can we truly understand
What it means to be human

freedom of fearlessness

Sometimes
I would wake
in the middle of the night
with so much to say
So many thoughts
rushing through my mind
I had to get them out
Or I would erupt
like the most volatile
of felsic volcanoes

Sleepless nights
spent writing
pages and documents
Entire collections
of streams of thought
like a flowing river
it's movement long and infinite
Until it merges with the ocean

But when the time came to speak
about the things that mattered
I always stayed silent
my voice
A mere person

trapped inside my head
not shown the door
to set itself free

Until the day
I found the key

An issue
of such significance
I could never stay silent again

- the dam that broke free

With ferocity
I acted
A sense of purpose
So blinding, but so liberating
All-consuming
I never looked back
Not even once

So driven
so ambitious
To create the change
I wished to be created

With every goal reached
I set a new one
Rising higher and higher

On the steps to my path

This engulfing, all-consuming passion
sense of purpose
Such powerful energy
Unstoppable, unbreakable

Once I am consumed by it
there is no holding me back
Because I have discovered
what it means
To be fearless

- breaking free from my limits

Living on the wildside
the thrill of it all
In love with the speed
Propelling me forward
as if I weigh nothing at all

My legs moving
long strides of effortless effort
Running so fast
my feet barely skimming the ground

Every time I tried to fly
I always found myself
in a bottomless pit

But now
I think I finally learned the secret

Grasping the handles
of a bike so sleek
As I soar down the steepest of hills
The wheels mere circles of black
blurred at the speed of light
The visible friction they leave behind
in their tracks
I'm soaring past
life as I know it
in its preparation for another day,
A new beginning
Transcending all limits of my body
with this simple machinery
That's allowing me to move
In ways I never have before

I love the drop
So quick, so fast
For just a single point in time
When I reach the top
I am weightless

And in that moment
I become wholly and inexpressibly
Free

- energy in motion

materialism and its
materializations

You say it's okay
to put your comforts
above all else
You say it's okay
to consume cruelty
You say it's okay
to have a little enjoyment in life
Enjoyment that comes at the cost
of others, always

If I was skinned
For the leather on your bag
Would you speak out against it?
Or would you be preoccupied
with an enjoyment
derived from suffering
Not a care in the world?

If I was given up control over my body
to those who wanted me
For my flesh, my milk
Maybe a trophy
to add to their collection
Would you speak out against it?

Or would you dismiss it
as a normal part
of a functioning society?

If I were bought and sold
stripped away from my mother,
my brothers and sisters
Would you speak out against it?
Or would you tell me
I'm an inferior being
That I don't deserve
your love and respect?

If I was forced through labor,
again and again,
every time
having my babies stolen away from me,
injected with drugs
So you can feast upon them
and upon my milk
Would you speak out against it?
Or would you allow
this cruelty to go on
blissfully ignorant,
At the cost of my suffering

You say
that I should be compassionate
You say

that I should be considerate
You say
that I should be intelligent

But tell me,
how can I learn
to be compassionate
when all that surrounds me is hate

How can I make
intelligent decisions
If all decisions made around me
Stem from a dysfunction
no sense of discrimination
Between right and wrong?

When will you learn
 to change
So your destructive practices
don't endanger the life around you?

Until then,
we can't see eye to eye
Or the whole world
will go blind

- call me an idealist, I stopped caring

How you so love

all that shines
Everything you call yours
reeks of seeming opulence
You drive your shiny cars
thinking you have made it
Turn on your fancy new appliance
Showing it off
because in it
Lies your self worth

Jealousy
got the best of you
Because your worth
lies in the external
in the everchanging

As soon as you think
you have made it
The requirements change on you
wind blowing it all away
All that you have gathered
gone
Now you're left
to pick up the pieces
And start anew

A new
type of success
Now you've bought

into the next trend
Changed the way you look
Shinier
you blend in
A cookie cutter
forming millions
just like you
But you still stand out
Not in a way that you like
You want to be like them
But you tell yourself
You're a leader
a trendsetter
You're no follower

Soon enough
the wind blows it all away
again
Truly lost now
Once unwavering
your confidence has broken
you hate the world
For it has been cruel to you

Little did you know
It's all been in your hands
this whole time
It's been your doing

Your understanding
of what matters
consequences unconsidered
Your own motives
of what's on the outside
Prized above all

Now
Your self worth shifts
to lie in the constant
to lie in you
You don't treasure
your shiny objects anymore
Little did you expect of it
but your life has changed
You love yourself deeply
and you can give others the same love
Your actions don't destroy
the world anymore
the planet, the animals, the people

They don't destroy you

You don't hate the world anymore
You hold it sacred
for all it has done for you
all it has taught you
Your frequency is love
Your energy is compassion

You spread it, radiate it
You let it course through you
Letting it become you
Until it is you

Your confidence pieces together
whole again
But you were never broken
only on the outside
Funny
Because that was the only place
you thought you were whole

And you rise
up
higher, higher, higher
Until you can't anymore

Not shiny on the outside
but you shine
Brighter than ever before

- illumination

lessons of a phoenix

I made the effort
I put in the time
I reached out
over and over
I sacrificed
my own well-being
because I thought I could preserve
what in my eyes
was beautiful

Every time I thought it could work
I raised my hopes
Only to be disappointed
Yet again
like unpicked fruit
Left to fall and wither

In it I realized
a relationship one-sided
Was all it could ever be
I thought my ways were right
honorable even
The preservation, continuation
of the old

But sometimes
that's all it was ever meant to be
remnants of the past
fragments, memories
Only existing in mind
to be drawn from
at will or need

Sometimes
what was in the past
Has to experience destruction
in the absolute sense
Has to burn to ashes
For the beautiful and new
to illuminate
The darkened caverns
of loneliest solitude

- lessons of broken friendships

Time
The ultimate healer
When I thought
I could never let go
For the hurt I felt
I could never let go
of the heavy weight
that pulled me under
I forgave

For the sake of us both

- forgiveness is power

When you said goodbye
I thought that was the end
but the end was never the end
it was only the beginning
of something beautiful and new

When cessation created continuity
And out of the ashes
of a perceivable end
arose a connection
that could only last a lifetime

- the end was never the end

new beginnings

In this morning
of new beginnings
As I take my first steps outside
I am immediately engulfed
in the early morning feeling
Like i'm being bathed
in the energy of serenity

The dewdrops on leaves
Seemingly crystallized into gems
Solid objects
that can be held and touched

The fog in the air
as it settles upon mountains so green
they can only be a mirage
Compelling, yet illusive
in their beauty

The smell of the air
Pure and crisp
In this moment
before it all begins
Nothing to pollute it with

The silence of this moment
All-encompassing
As if the world
is holding its breath
For the turbulence that is about to begin

beautiful moments

We count the raindrops
one by one
As they slowly dissolve into nothingness
And leave behind remnants
a beautiful wet feeling of satisfaction
on our tongues

We watch our footprints in the sand
side by side
One set long, deep
In it
carrying centuries of wisdom
One set small, shallow
A palette open to receiving
becoming increasingly filled
With the fleeting knowledge of life

We followed the paths paved for us
excited to learn
what those before us had
A telltale of adventure and discovery
of all that preceded

But in our expression
we carved the way

for a path beautiful and new
We lit the dark road
with the lanterns of our discovery

The means for understanding
for those who would be lost
in the otherwise vast terrains
Of a great world

- footprints of discovery

We walked for hours
in the sun
in the rain
Under the stars
with only moonlight to light our path
not a care
for what the elements had in store for us

We talked for hours
about the nonsensical and sensical alike
with the mountains and forest to aid us
in conversations that felt significant
Light hearted
but awash with meaning

We hiked up the mountains
into the sunset
and basking in the golden light

seeing and seen
by the crimson-red sky
We had found the meaning we sought
A meaning
that could never be put into words
A sensation
ever so fleeting as sensations are
But a feeling, long lasting

Both young and small
so insignificant
yet so important
In a world infinitely larger than us

- beneath a scarlet sky

In that moment
of truest connection
I faded into you
and you into me
Like the ocean mist
into the morning sky
Maybe some people
are just meant to be
In the same story

wanderings of the mind

Maybe we're all lost
and we're trying to find our way back home
Like wanderers of the world
our instruments of perception outward bound
Our states of perpetual lostness
manifesting themselves in infinitely different
ways

Maybe we're afraid
Of how truly powerful we are
of our power
As it rushes through us
a blinding but awakening force
So we numb it
Over and over
with the stimulation
Of the world around us
trapped under a facade
of weakness
So we never have to face the reality
of our strength

Maybe we look for validation
in other people, situations
Because we're not secure

in ourselves
And swimming in this insecurity
Life becomes the thing
that happens to us
while we're off
In our self-created worlds

Maybe our moments
of boredom and nothingness
Are simple expressions
Our way of finding
what it means to be at peace

Maybe instead of being receptive
we resist against everything that's new
Because we're so afraid of being hurt
that vulnerability isn't an option
And we remain fragments of potential
trapped inside a body

Maybe underneath
all the superficial
conformities
We are all crazy
Because whose strange notion
Was 'normal'
 in the first place?

Maybe the cookie cutter houses

In all their suburbia
are a mere reflection
an outward manifestation
Of the unattainable ideal
we work so hard to attain

And our education system
is a factory
That is producing a whole generation
of complacent individuals
Who know only
how to memorize textbooks
and follow directions
Who are increasingly being diagnosed
victimized for all their faults

Because our conceptions of 'normal'
only gave us one way to learn
A way that killed the fire of curiosity
at an age so young

Maybe we just need to be found
rescued
From ourselves
and the world we create
An outward manifestation
Of our inner states of being

Or

We were beautiful all along
exactly how we were meant to be
And it is ideas of wrongdoing
The constant reiteration
of imperfection
An eternal state
of not-enoughness
that created the systems
we live by and die by

Maybe there never was
right and wrong
and the only mistake at all
Was telling ourselves
that there was one
And beyond notions
of right and wrong
there is a vast space
that holds the answerless answers we seek

- the trek back home

The illuminator and illumination
Inseparable
And in it
The dichotomy
Of the perceiver and perceived

Simply a fabrication

To be experienced
In this world of separation

What if we faded
into each other
And became nothing at all?

External circumstances
material objects
Only hold power over us
because of what we feel within
What if
we eliminated
The middle man
And within the seat of experience
We experienced the emotion itself
Untainted, unaffected
by anything that changes

Like an alchemist
of our inner states of being
Transmuting the unwanted
into the beautiful

How powerful
Would that be?

- thought experiments

And I'm off
chasing another dream
from my wildest fantasies
Hoping for one second
a single moment
I can find such intensity in my life
A single pointed focus so strong
That I need no purpose
beyond my own

Hoping that
for one second
I can feel emotion so deep
I am transcended
into a whole different dimension
Of pure awareness

Hoping that
even for a single point in time
the most fleeting of moments
Where time and space are one
The moment
between stimulus and response
where my will is completely free
I have wandered upon
what it means
To be
completely and entirely at peace

- wanderlust

a universal language

All of us so different
in our communication
The words we speak
like bricks to build bridges
The languages we speak them in
ever so complex

The way we open up
Some people open-books
ready to be read
at any given moment
Others
only vulnerable
when they feel safe, protected

The way we express emotion
Some people
letting it all out
before it festers like a sore
Others
holding it all in
until it's ready to burst free
Others yet
acknowledging it, addressing it
before it even has the chance
to spiral into something more

The way we show gratitude
The way we hold it in
The way we express love freely
The way we save it for those
we think matter the most

But in all our infinite languages
and their expressions
The language of love
compassion
suffering and sadness
anger and loneliness
playfulness and lightheartedness
The entire spectrum of human emotion
universal as it is
can be understood by us all
Without a single utterance

- a language without words

Lost in the music
Emotions so raw, so real
Unimaginably so
Yet completely unreal

The sadness, the longing
a place of unexplainable depth
So heavy, so impactful
a force with no weight
Something to contemplate and ponder

Something to get lost in
The gravity of it all
the inner workings, the intelligence

Emotions so powerful
I'm transported to another dimension
of pure feeling
All the words
taken out of me
and I'm truly lost
In the beauty of a feeling
Eons old
and yet so new, timeless
So unique
to this moment
Only

This emotion
Pure energy
Untethered, untied
to the circumstantial, experiential
Always there
to be called upon

A spectrum infinite and universal
in both intensity and frequency
Beauty can only be appreciated
through understanding

- when vibrational motion was propagated

it was in me all along

She thought
there was much to be done
Associating herself
with the chaos
Because she loved the motion

She thought
She could find freedom
in it all
The wanderings and the happenings
The action and the service

She thought
If she traveled the world
If she discovered all that was new
If she learned all there was to absorb
She could be the possessor
of ultimate knowledge
And with this attainment
She could awaken
And be truly content

What she didn't know
Was that
there was never anything

To be done

Every inch of her skin
held the ancient stories of time

Every space in her body
held the potential for origination
Of the most creative of expression
Every bone in her skeletal structure
was the manifestation
of unimaginable strength

And sitting in stillness
she found infinitely more
than she ever dreamed of
When she traveled the world

metamorphosis

The lonely mounds of sand
Washed over
by waves of the ocean
Until what is left
Has transformed
into something completely new

In it
Carrying untold stories
of struggle and suffering
But only what has endured
can last

- a powerful transformation

The gem that arose
from the most extreme
Of struggle and pressure
And the longest cycles
of millennia

A single element
buried deep under
a surface of immense weight

For all its coarseness, imperfections
rough edges
The light still found a way
to shine through

Emanating
such effervescent beauty
despite outward chaos

For even diamonds
cannot be polished

- shine bright like a diamond

wild and free

Meet me at the horizon
Where the sun and sky
fade into land and sea
Where the moon and stars
dissolve into the innocent
light of day
Like a lover's kiss

The place where
nothing and everything converge
Into absolute dissolution

Where I finally crossed
the ocean of my mind
As the steerer of seas
tranquil and turbulent alike

Where I bathed
in the wildest of my imagination
the most unrealistic of ideals
Untainted by fear
in the purest sense
And basking in this newfound light

I ran free

ACKNOWLEDGEMENT

To all the people who have stayed true to your journey and spoken your truth, thank you for paving the path for the rest of us to follow in your footsteps. And to all those whose everyday journey feels like an uphill battle, thank you for finding the strength and courage to face each challenge; you truly are an inspiration.

I would like to express gratitude for all the people I have been lucky to meet in my life, and have the fortune of calling a friend—you know who you are. Your compassion, support, and ability to tolerate my constant thirst for adventure means so much to me.

Thank you to my parents, who were always supportive, always there for me no matter the situation, and who taught me that education and self-determination would set me free. It is with your guidance that I have evolved into the person I am today.

And lastly, thank you to my sister for always being there for me. You are the most dependable, supportive, and caring person I know, and I'm excited to continue creating a lifetime of memories with you.